Maine
Now and Then

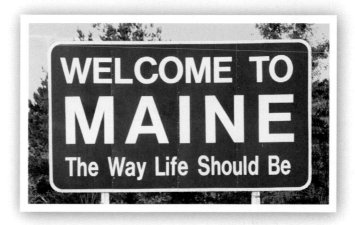

WELCOME TO
MAINE
The Way Life Should Be

by Sheila Sweeny Higginson

Scott Foresman
is an imprint of

PEARSON

Glenview, Illinois • Boston, Massachusetts • Chandler, Arizona
Upper Saddle River, New Jersey

Illustration 6 Steve Toole

Photographs
Every effort has been made to secure permission and provide appropriate credit for photographic material. The publisher deeply regrets any omission and pledges to correct errors called to its attention in subsequent editions.

Unless otherwise acknowledged, all photographs are the property of Pearson Education, Inc.

Photo locators denoted as follows: Top (T), Center (C), Bottom (B), Left (L), Right (R), Background (Bkgd)

CVR © Michael P. Gadomski/SuperStock; **1** ©Visions of America, LLC/Alamy; **3** © Chad Ehlers/Alamy Images; **5** © Michael P. Gadomski/SuperStock; **7** ©Visions of America, LLC/Alamy; **8** © 2000-2006 Sanford Historical Committee/Maine Historical Society; **9** © Carl D. Walsh/Getty Images; **11** (Bkgd) © 2000-2006 Patten Lumbermen's Museum/ Maine Historical Society, (Inset) Corbis; **12** © 2000-2006 Maine Historical Society; **13** ©NewsCom; **14** Smithsonian American Art Museum, Washington, DC/Art Resource, NY; **16** © Peter Adams Photography/Alamy Images; **17** Ezra Shaw/Getty Images; **18** (B) Corbis, (T) ©Visions of America, LLC/Alamy; **19** ©Visions of America, LLC/Alamy.

ISBN 13: 978-0-328-51654-4
ISBN 10:   0-328-51654-6

4 5 6 7 8 9 10 V0FL 14 13 12 11

Every morning, people in one state in the United States get to see the sunrise before anyone else in the country. That's because they live in Maine, the easternmost of all the fifty states. Maine is located on the rocky coast of the Atlantic Ocean between the southern boundaries of the Canadian provinces of Quebec and New Brunswick. The state is known today for its lobsters, potatoes, and blueberries; its ships and lighthouses; and for its evergreen forests.

In fact, Maine is known as "The Pine Tree State." Both its state tree and state flower are the white pine with its cone and tassel. But there is much more to know about this forested state where many city people go to enjoy the quiet beauty of nature.

Maine's majestic coastline at sunrise

Maine was home to the first non-Native American colony in New England. It was called the Popham Colony, and it was formed by settlers from England in the summer of 1607—thirteen years before the Pilgrims began their settlement in Massachusetts. The settlers at Popham soon learned that Maine life was not easy; the colony lasted only a little more than a year.

The Land

When the Popham settlers first landed in Maine, they looked upon a magnificent, **untamed** wilderness. Glaciers had carved the coastline during the last Ice Age thousands of years before. The rocky coastline, the rivers, and the lakes of Maine are what the glaciers left behind as they **thawed** and retreated north. The glacial retreat also formed the thousands of islands that are found in Atlantic waters off the coast of Maine.

Some of Maine's most notable **features** then were its forests full of pine, spruce, and birch trees. Today they remain an important state resource. Although many trees were cut down as the logging industry boomed in the 1800s, more than 80 percent of the state is still covered with forests. This is why Maine is known as the Pine Tree State.

The cliffs of Maine's coast are popular with hikers.

The People

Who were the first people to live in Maine? No one knows for sure. Scientists believe that Ice Age hunters arrived there as early as ten thousand years ago. But the first group there is evidence of is the "Red Paint" people. Scientists don't know much about them except that they lined their graves with red clay and lived in Maine about five thousand years ago.

Many Native American tribes were living in Maine when the first European settlers arrived.

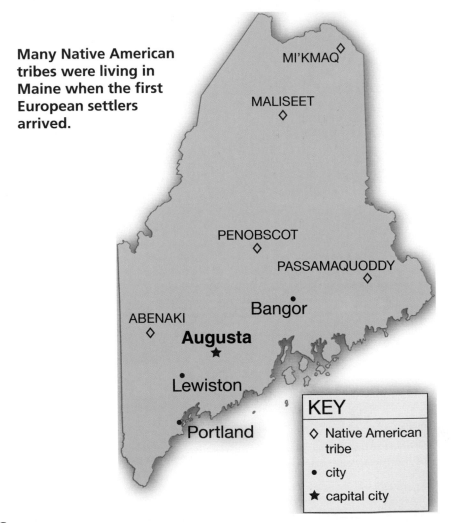

KEY

◇ Native American tribe

● city

★ capital city

By the time the Popham settlers arrived, dozens of Native American tribes were living in the area. Most were part of the Wabanaki Nation and included the Mi'kmaq, Abenaki, Maliseet, Passamaquoddy, and Penobscot tribes. Some, like the Abenaki, farmed the land, while others, like the Mi'kmaq, were nomadic hunters and gatherers. All of their lives changed dramatically when European settlers arrived. Today, the five tribes have reservations in Maine. They continue to practice their tribal traditions and are represented as nonvoting members in the state legislature.

The descendants of the early English, Scottish, and Irish settlers in Maine are sometimes called Yankees. People of French descent also have a strong presence in the state, many of whom traveled from Canada to work in the logging industry. Maine's population has grown slowly compared to other states in the Northeast; it is the least-populated state east of the Mississippi River. Most people live in the southwest part of the state, and about half live in urban areas around the cities of Portland, Lewiston, Bangor, and Augusta, the capital.

Farming

There is an old joke about farming in Maine. A farmer is busy sowing his field when a stranger approaches. The stranger asks, "What are you growing?" The farmer replies, "Rocks."

Maine's soil is indeed rocky, and the weather can be extreme, so meeting the **requirements** for successful farming is a big challenge. But that didn't stop the people of Maine from making agriculture an important industry. Native Americans **harnessed** the land to grow crops such as corn, beans, and squash, and the early settlers relied on farming to feed their families. Many family farms were replaced after the Civil War, when larger commercial farms focused on growing crops such as corn and potatoes and producing dairy products.

Although challenging, farming was a big industry.

Maine is known today for its potatoes, blueberries, apples, and dairy products. It is also known for its seafood "crops," particularly lobsters.

Canning of farm products was once a huge business in Maine. At the beginning of the twentieth century, Maine had 175 canneries that hired thousands of workers every fall. Most of those factories closed down by the 1960s, though, because of the increasing emphasis on frozen and fresh, year-round food and also because of competing canneries in other parts of the country.

Maine lobsters are famous worldwide.

9

Logging

Where there are forests full of trees, you will usually find a thriving lumber industry. Logging started in the 1600s in Maine, and since that time, the state's trees have been used for everything from building ships to making the pages of books.

The first sawmill in America was built in Maine in 1623 on the Piscataqua River. Over the next two hundred years, Maine became one of the largest lumber shippers in the world. In the mid-1800s, thousands of **lumberjacks** lived in logging camps. They worked in crews to cut down trees and float the logs down the Penobscot River. Once the logs reached the mills in Bangor, Maine, they were used to make lumber or paper.

The logging industry has declined since its boom period at the turn of the twentieth century, but it is still alive and well. Today, Maine trees are largely used for furniture, to make pulp for paper products, and for specialty boats. Logging continues to produce billions of dollars in state revenue each year.

Logging was dangerous and difficult work.

Shipbuilding

Ships were needed to sail to Maine from Europe and back again. In fact, during the year they lived in Maine, the Popham colony settlers built the *Virginia*, a thirty-ton ship that they sailed back to England. The *Virginia* was the first ship built and launched in the Western Hemisphere. It was one of many thousands built in Maine, where both wood and master shipbuilders were plentiful.

Some of the greatest ships on the sea were built in Maine. Custom yachts and sailboats are still being built in Maine today (right).

Like logging, shipbuilding was not an occupation for the weak or lazy. The men who worked in the shipyards had to be both strong and skilled. Their days were long, their wages were low, and they had no paid vacations or holidays. But they can be credited with building some of the most majestic vessels ever built.

At the beginning of the twentieth century, wooden ships began to be replaced by ships built of iron and steel. Although Maine's boat builders are not as busy as they once were, they are still known for making custom yachts and sailboats and even most canoes built in the United States.

The Arts

Maine has been home to many famous artists and writers. Some, like the poet Henry Wadsworth Longfellow, were born in Maine and later moved to other places. In the 1800s, Longfellow was one of the most popular American poets.

Harriet Beecher Stowe wasn't born in Maine, but she wrote her memorable book, *Uncle Tom's Cabin*, while she lived in the state. The book's story of the horrible conditions of enslaved people in the United States helped to spread the message that slavery was **unnatural** and should end. President Lincoln told Stowe that her book had been a big factor in causing the Civil War.

Landscape painter Winslow Homer lived in a fishing village on the coast of Maine. The sea and the people who worked along the coast inspired several of Homer's realistic paintings.

High Cliff, Coast of Maine by Winslow Homer

Many famous children's authors wrote their most popular books in Maine. Among them are E. B. White, who wrote *Charlotte's Web* and *Stuart Little* there, and Robert McCloskey, who lived in Maine and wrote *Blueberries for Sal* and *One Morning in Maine.*

Tourism

Millions of tourists flock to Maine each year to gaze at the fall foliage that brightens the 17 million acres of forest in the state. At that time of year, the leaves turn dazzling shades of yellow, orange, and red. This painted landscape can be seen throughout the state—driving along the winding roads or hiking through the mountains. Many "leaf peepers" travel to Acadia National Park on Mount Desert Island; it is the second-most-visited national park in the United States. Leaves are at their colorful peak the last week in September and the first week in October.

Maine's fall foliage is spectacular.

Ski areas draw many tourists in winter.

Once the leaves have fallen and the ground is covered with snow, Maine becomes a winter wonderland for people who enjoy winter activities. With an average yearly snowfall of sixty to ninety inches, Maine boasts more than a dozen Alpine, or downhill, ski areas. The state also has countless pristine trails for advanced and beginning skiers. Many ski areas also offer snowboarding, snowshoeing, snowmobiling, and cross-country skiing for adventurous visitors.

During the spring and summer months, tourists continue to flood the state by the millions. Many come to see the more than sixty historic lighthouses that dot the state's shoreline. Farther from the coast, whitewater rafting and kayaking are popular ways to explore Maine's rivers and streams. And those ready for a challenge can tackle Mt. Katahdin. At 5,267 feet, it is Maine's tallest peak.

A Changing Maine

When Maine became the twenty-third state in 1820, the population was about three hundred thousand people. It is four times as large now, at just over 1.3 million. Mighty industries such as fishing and shipbuilding once ruled the state. Although they still exist, other businesses, such as increased lumber production and tourism, have taken the lead. Cities have sprouted and have spread out into suburbs.

Maine continues to change and grow.

VIEW IN CONGRESS STREET, PORTLAND.

But the best of Maine has stayed the same. Majestic forests still blanket the state, and ocean waves crash on its jagged shores. Untouched rural areas and small towns greatly outnumber the few larger cities. And the people of Maine continue to take pride in their state and have a deep connection to the magnificent land they call home.

The sign at the border between Kittery, Maine, and New Hampshire is an **announcement** of how many Mainers feel. It says: "Welcome to Maine: The Way Life Should Be."

Glossary

announcement *n.* act of announcing or making known

feature *n.* a distinct part or quality

harnessed *v.* controlled or put to use

lumberjacks *n.* people whose work is cutting down trees

requirements *n.* things that are needed

thawed *v.* to have melted ice, snow, or anything frozen

unnatural *adj.* not natural; not normal

untamed *adj.* wild; not obedient